PARANORMAL HANDBOOKS

HANDBOOK TO

BIGFOOT, NESSIE,

AND

OTHER UNEXPLAINED CREATURES

BY TYLER OMOTH

CAPSTONE PRESS

a capstone imprint

Edge Books are published by Capstone Press,
1710 Roe Crest Drive, North Mankato, Minnesota 56003.
www.mycapstonepub.com

Library of Congress Cataloging-in-Publication Data
Names: Omoth, Tyler, author.
Title: Handbook to Bigfoot, Nessie, and other unexplained creatures / by
   Tyler Omoth.
Description: North Mankato, Minnesota : Capstone Press, 2017. | Series: Edge
   books. Paranormal handbooks | Includes bibliographical references and
   index. | Audience: Age 9–12. | Audience: Grade 4 to 6.
Identifiers: LCCN 2016004345 | ISBN 9781515713111 (library binding) | ISBN
   9781515713159 (ebook (pdf))
Subjects: LCSH: Monsters—Juvenile literature. | Animals, Mythical.
Classification: LCC GR825 .O66 2017 | DDC 001.944—dc23
LC record available at http://lccn.loc.gov/2016004345

Editorial Credits
Nate LeBoutillier, editor; Philippa Jenkins, designer; Svetlana Zhurkin, media researcher;
Kathy McColley, production specialist

Photo Credits
Alamy: Mary Evans Picture Library, 24, Universal Art Archive, 16; AP Photo: Charleston Daily
Mail/Craig Cunningham, 23, Eric Gay, 19 (bottom); Getty Images: Hulton Archive, 25, Nisian
Hughes, cover (bottom), Stringer/Ian Tyas, 12, The Washington Post/Amanda Voisard, 22;
iStockphoto: Andrew Rich, 6, Vaara, cover (top), back cover, yanishka, 8; Library of Congress,
21; Mary Evans Picture Library, 20; Newscom: ZUMA Press/Keystone Pictures USA, 13,
ZUMA Press/Vince Talotta, 7; Shutterstock: Alexlky, 18, Atelier Sommerland, 17, BestGreen-
Screen, 1, 29, Eric Isselee, 27, Fer Gregory, 28, Francois Loubser, 10—11, GROGL, 5, Mar-
clSchauer, 19 (top), Mike H, 4, Reno Martin, 9, rudall30, 14, Shafran, 15, SvedOliver, 26

Design Elements by Shutterstock

Printed and bound in China.
007721

TABLE OF CONTENTS

Searching for Mysterious Creatures

Every now and then humans see glimpses of mysterious animals. People have reported seeing apelike creatures at the edges of forests. Giant lizards, like leftovers from the time of dinosaurs, reportedly roam waterways. From mermaids to frog-men, stories of wonderful and hidden creatures have been told throughout hundreds of years. But are they real, and if so, are they dangerous?

Is it possible that some of these beasts, monsters, and amazing creatures exist? Today many believe these creatures, called **cryptids**, are just stories made up for amusement. But others take these stories very seriously.

Will **cryptozoology** ever prove the existence of any of these creatures? No one knows for sure. But until then, people need to keep their eyes open at all times. One might catch a glimpse of a hairy, humanlike creature in the woods or a beast that belongs in a time long forgotten.

cryptid—any creature that may or may not exist
crytpozoology—the search for and study of creatures whose existence or survival is disputed

From California up the coast and into Canada, people report a strange creature roaming the forests. Since the early 1800s, local settlers have found footprints in the mud that span more than 15 inches (38 centimeters) long. Hikers and residents claim they've seen the beast that left the footprints behind too. It's taller than an average man. Some witnesses say it stands up to 9 feet (2.74 meters) tall. It walks like a human, but it's covered in hair like an ape. If the creature is real, is it man, or is it beast? Or might it be a bit of both?

Before white settlers moved into North America, American Indians had their own tales of the beast. In 1920 Canadian journalist J.W. Burns collected their stories of the creature. He called the beast "Sasquatch," based on the Salish word *Sesquac* which means "wild man." In one account, Burns quotes a young woman named Emma Paul who said, "I saw the Sasquatch a few yards from the house ... He was very big and powerful in appearance."

In 1958 a California newspaper, *The Humboldt Times*, ran a story after hearing about a giant set of footprints found at a construction site. In the article they named the beast responsible "Bigfoot." The footprints turned out to be a **hoax**. The 1958 newspaper story was one of many hoaxes related to the legendary beast.

Researcher Christopher Lau holds a cast of an alleged Bigfoot track.

hoax—a trick to make people believe something that is not true

Photos and videos that claim to show Bigfoot but cannot be **verified** as real add confusion. Are they real or not? No one has ever captured Bigfoot, so he still remains a mystery.

The legend of Bigfoot is still popular today. Documentaries about Bigfoot are plentiful. The creature has even turned up in some movies, such as *Harry and the Hendersons* and *Hotel Transylvania*. In Willow Creek, California, citizens celebrate Big Foot Days every September with games and a parade held in Sasquatch's honor.

verify—to make sure that something is true

Creature Feature

Yeti   Sometimes called "The Abominable Snowman," the Yeti is a white, apelike creature that is said to live in the Himalayas.

Skunk Ape   This Bigfoot-like creature supposedly hides in the swamps of Florida and the southeastern United States. It emits an odor similar to rotten eggs.

Yowie   Similar to Bigfoot, the Yowie has thick black or dark brown fur. It is said to live in the wilderness of Australia.

Almas   More human-like than apelike, these creatures are covered with red-brown hair. They reportedly live in Russia and Mongolia.

WARNING BIGFOOT ZONE

NESSIE

In the highlands of Scotland lies a body of freshwater called Loch Ness. It measures 23 miles (36 km) long and is up to 1,000 feet (305 m) deep in some parts. Many people believe that within those depths, the Loch Ness Monster makes its home. "Nessie," as the locals call the monster, is said to be up to 30 feet (9.1 m) long with a long neck, two sets of flippers, and a humped back. Some reports say it has two or three humps. It looks like a large, swimming dinosaur.

An engineer named Tim Dinsdale who was boating out in the Loch in 1960 claims to have caught sight of Nessie. "It came out like a black snake," he said. "Like a black anaconda, that's what it looked like. It came out like that and then it went down and it was a boil of white foam." Dinsdale managed to get several seconds of his **encounter** on film. Scientists studied that film for decades, but have not determined if it is real.

encounter—an unexpected or difficult meeting

In 1969 a Loch Ness investigation team kept a close watch at all times.

Over the last century, dozens of photos and videos have continued to pop up. Regardless, there is still no **conclusive** evidence that Nessie exists. Some think Nessie is some sort of dinosaur that has managed to stay alive and hidden for centuries. Others believe it's just a figment of people's imagination.

Search teams went to great depths to find Nessie, as this submarine launched in 1969 shows.

conclusive—serving to settle a question; convincing

Real or not, Nessie has captured the fancy of people around the world. The movie *The Water Horse* is an entertaining account of how Nessie came to be in the Loch. References to Nessie also pop up in songs, TV shows, and literature. You can even ride the Loch Ness Monster rollercoaster at Busch Gardens in Williamsburg, Virginia.

Sneaky Snapshot

The most famous photo of the Loch Ness Monster was reportedly taken on April 19, 1934, by Colonel Robert Wilson. After its circulation, the photo caused a stir. Some thought it looked like the head of a dinosaur, an otter, or some other unknown sea serpent. In 1994 it was revealed that Nessie was, in fact, a toy submarine outfitted with a false sea serpent head. But some people don't believe it's fake.

The most famous photo of the Loch Ness Monster first appeared in 1934.

MERMAIDS

Exhausted and often hungry, explorers on the high seas would catch a glimpse of something. Was that a woman in the ocean? No, it had a tail like a fish. Even Christopher Columbus reported seeing mermaids in his travel journals from 1493. He wrote, "They were not as beautiful as they are painted, although to some extent they have a human appearance in the face."

Mermaids appear in the **mythology** of many cultures. In art they are often beautiful women with long, elegant tails much like that of a very large salmon. Reported sightings have frequently been less flattering. They seem to pose little danger as most reports refer to them as shy and a little playful.

In 2009 Schlomo Cohen, a young man in Israel, reported seeing a mermaid. "At first I thought she was just another sunbather, but when we approached, she jumped into the water and disappeared. We were all in shock because we saw she had a tail." The local government offered a $1-million reward for proof of the mermaid's existence.

mythology—old stories told again and again that help connect people with their past

Are mermaids real creatures resulting from **evolution**? Might they be aliens? Perhaps exhausted sailors and tourists are mistaking other sea creatures such as otters or manatees for mermaids.

Maybe mermaids are mythical creatures. Maybe mermaids are cases of mistaken identity. Whatever the truth, it's worth keeping an eye on the water in case an authentic mermaid is lurking nearby.

evolution—the gradual changing of living things over a long period of time

FREAKY FACT

Even the great writer, William Shakespeare, was fascinated by mermaids. He wrote of a character seeing a mermaid riding a dolphin's back in his comedy, *A Midsummer Night's Dream.*

CHUPACABRA

an artistic picture of Chupacabra

Reports of the Chupacabra depict a frightening creature. It is said to stand about 5 feet (1.5 m) tall and have large, alien-like eyes, long fangs, and long spikes down its back. Its suspected victims, usually livestock or small animals, are discovered dead and drained of all blood with bite marks.

Chupacabra is Spanish for "goat-sucker." The first accounts of its appearance came in 1995 in Puerto Rico. A local farmer found eight of his sheep dead in the night and drained of their blood. Later that year, approximately 150 different animals died in similar conditions. Reports of the attacks reached other countries where similar attacks occurred. The legend of the Chupacabra was born.

The okapi has stripes like a zebra but is most closely related to the giraffe.

Myth-Like Creatures

Sometimes the mysterious and unexplained does get explained. Several mysterious creatures thought to be legend have turned out to be very real animals. The duck-billed platypus, the okapi, and the Komodo Dragon were all once thought to be the stuff of myths.

There is no video of the Chupacabra, and few photos exist. No one has captured one. Eyewitnesses swear by what they saw. The mysterious deaths of animals drained of blood make the existence of a vampire-like animal roaming the Americas all too possible.

Phylis Canion holds a photo of an animal that turned up dead outside her ranch in Cuero, Texas, in 2007. She believed it was the Chupacabra.

Could it be coyotes, or is there something more sinister out there? Whether or not the beast is real, the mystery of the Chupacabra is alive and well.

07/14/2007

THE JERSEY DEVIL

Few monsters have struck fear into local residents the way The Jersey Devil has in the Pine Barrens area of New Jersey. In 1909 the sightings were so common that schools closed and men formed **posses** to protect themselves.

The story says that in 1735 a New Jersey woman named Deborah Leeds gave birth to her 13th child. During childbirth, she invoked the name of the devil. When her child was born, he transformed into a demonic monster with a horse's head, bat wings, long thin legs, and a reptilian tail. He escaped through the chimney and has been haunting the area ever since.

simple drawing of
The Jersey Devil

posse—a group of people gathered to find and co a suspect

the Leeds House
in New Jersey

No one has been able to capture The Jersey Devil, and it is said that police dogs refuse to follow its footprints. Whether the people of New Jersey are cursed with this part demon or not, you can still hear mothers warning their children, "Don't be out late, or The Jersey Devil may get you!"

FREAKY FACT

In 1982 New Jersey got its first National Hockey League team. A fan contest produced the New Jersey Devils as the team name in honor of the Jersey Devil legend.

MOTHMAN

In 1966 a few men were digging a grave at a cemetery by Clendenin, West Virginia. They claimed that they saw something in the trees. It was like a man, but it was large and brown. Then it spread large wings before sailing over their heads. Soon other sightings of the strange creature were reported, and the legend of the Mothman was born.

"The Legend of the Mothman" statue by Bob Roach stands in Pointe Pleasant, West Virginia.

interior of the Mothman Museum in West Virginia

After the first sighting, most reports of the Mothman were centered around the area of an old factory plant near Pointe Pleasant, West Virginia. The story of the second sighting involves a woman named Marcella Bennett. One night she and her daughter returned home from an errand and were startled by a creature near her car. "It seemed as though it had been lying down," she reported. "It rose up slowly from the ground. A big, gray thing. Bigger than a man with terrible, glowing eyes."

Soon mysterious men dressed in black suits arrived in the area, questioning local residents. Were they secret government agents looking for an alien?

Occasional sightings still happen, and the legend of the Mothman is as strong as ever in the Pointe Pleasant area.

FREAKY FACT

Clendenin, West Virginia, has a Mothman Museum and holds an annual Mothman festival each September. Many visitors take photos with a famous statue of the beast.

SPRING-HEELED JACK

Not all mysterious cryptids appear entirely monstrous. In the case of the Spring-Heeled Jack, he appeared dressed as a proper gentleman. Reports of the Spring-Heeled Jack first popped up in 1837 near London, England. He would appear quite suddenly, startling people before escaping by leaping over tall walls.

In 1838 two separate accounts reported that he attacked women. In each report the victim said that he spit blue flame at their face to stun them. Another account of a Spring-Heeled Jack attack came in 1877. A man in a long **cloak** approached an army guard. When he was close enough, the mysterious man slapped the guard. Though the guard shot at the stranger, the bullets had no effect. The man leapt over the guard and bounded off in great strides. The mysterious creature became popular in plays and writings of the time.

cloak—a loose piece of clothing that is used like a coat or cape

Spring-Heeled Jack reports popped up again in the 1970s and 1980s. He always appeared wearing a dark cloak or jacket, he slapped people, and he escaped by leaping over very tall walls. Though instructed to find him, police never identified or apprehended the Spring-Heeled Jack.

THE LOVELAND FROGMEN

Late at night while driving down a country road in 1955, residents of Loveland, Ohio, saw strange beings by the roadside. They stood about 4 feet (1.21 m) tall and had leathery skin, webbed feet, and heads like giant frogs. One witness reported seeing one of the creatures raise a wand with sparks flying out of it. A strong odor of alfalfa and almonds hung in the air. These are the Loveland Frogmen.

Almost 20 years later in the same area near the banks of the Ohio River, a police officer made an emergency stop. He had swerved to avoid hitting what looked like a giant frog. The creature stood up and ran away on two feet like a man. Two weeks later, another officer reported seeing and shooting a similar creature. This officer, however, later changed his story, saying that it was just a large, escaped house pet.

The sightings were detailed enough to make local police and even the Federal Bureau of Investigation (FBI) come to the area to check it out. Though they did find some tracks, they could never prove the existence of the Loveland Frogmen.

HANDBOOK QUIZ

1. Which creature often jumps out and surprises people by slapping them?

a. Bear Lake Monster
b. Spring-Heeled Jack
c. The Kraken
d. Beast of Bulgaria

2. Which creature had a stage musical made about them?

a. Jackalope
b. Wolf Boy of West Egg
c. Old Yellow Top
d. Loveland Frogman

3. Which cryptid draws over a million tourists to its location each year?

a. Nessie
b. Kumi Lizard
c. Devil Hawk
d. Maltese Tiger

4. Which creature was mentioned in Christopher Columbus' journal?

a. Fireborn Phoenix
b. Moby Dick
c. Mermaid
d. Wave Warrior Dave

5. Which creature is known for sucking the blood from its victims?

a. Fezzik the Fox
b. Chupacabra
c. Zombie Dingo
d. Spring Grove Serpent

Answers: 1-b, 2-d, 3-a, 4-c, 5-b.

GLOSSARY

cloak (KLOHK)—a loose piece of clothing that is used like a coat or cape

conclusive (kuhn-CLOO-siv)—serving to settle a question; convincing

cryptid (KRYP-tid)—any creature that may or may not exist

cryptozoology (kyp-toh-zoo-AHL-uh-jee)—the search for and study of creatures whose existence or survival is disputed

encounter (en-KOUN-tur)—an unexpected or difficult meeting

evolution (ev-uh-LOO-shun)—the gradual changing of living things over a long period of time

hoax (HOHKS)—to trick to make people believe something that is not true

mythology (mi-THOL-uh-jee)—old stories told again and again that help connect people with their past

posse (POSS-ee)—a group of people gathered to catch a suspect

verify (VAIR-ih-fye)—to make sure that something is true

READ MORE

Hile, Lori. *The Loch Ness Monster*. Solving Mysteries With Science. Chicago, Capstone Raintree, 2013.

Johnson, Hal, and Tom Mead. *Fearsome Creatures of the Lumberwoods: 20 Chilling Tales from the Wilderness*. New York: Workman Publishing, 2015.

Peterson, Megan C. *Encountering Chupacabra and Other Cryptids: Eyewitness Accounts*. Eyewitness to the Unexplained. North Mankato, Minn.: Capstone Press, 2014.

INTERNET SITES

FactHound offers a safe, fun way to find Internet sites related to this book. All of the sites on FactHound have been researched by our staff.

Here's all you do:

Visit *www.facthound.com*

Type in this code: 9781515713111

Check out projects, games and lots more at
www.capstonekids.com

Super-cool stuff!

INDEX